F$CK YOU
MONEY

HOW TO PLAY THE GAME OF MONEY BY YOUR OWN RULES, TRAVEL THE WORLD IN STYLE AND LIVE A LIFE OF FREEDOM, PROSPERITY & FINANCIAL CONTROL

Ray Bolden

F$CK YOU MONEY
Copyright © 2019 Ray Bolden. All rights reserved.

The book you are about to read is based on the experience of its author, Ray Bolden as well as information he has read or come in contact with. Mr. Bolden does not hold any legal, accounting, or college degrees nor does he or has he ever held a securities license.

Disclaimer

This publication is designed to provide accurate and authoritative information in regard to the subject matter covered. It is sold with the understanding that neither the author nor the publisher is engaged in rendering legal, investment, accounting or other professional advice. Any actions with regard to the information contained in this book should be undertaken only with the advice and counsel of a trained legal professional. If legal advice or other expert assistance is required, the services of a competent professional person should be sought.

The entire project is underwritten by the author. His views and interpretations of the findings may not necessarily be the same as those of the organizations that market the brands that are mentioned in this work.

ISBN-13: 978-0-578-49137-0 (Bold Ambition Worldwide, LLC)
ISBN-10: 0-578-49137-0

Dedication

This is dedicated to my mentor-in-the-mirror. You were right about everything. Thanks for always reflecting my full potential and for the intellectual thoughts and rebellious conversations that taught me how to play my own game within the game...we did it again!!!

Author's Note

Shape the world to adapt to you, not the other way around.

Table of Contents

Preface

For those who are not familiar, another type of American Dream has developed. The freedom to turn over your desk, shoot a bird at your boss, and retire on the spot without making a lifestyle sacrifice. How many times have you wanted to say fuck you to your boss...fuck this job and have the freedom to do what you want? *F$CK YOU MONEY* is the wealth mindset that you need to buy your freedom, so that you can choose to work or not to work, start a company, or just say 'fuck you' to your boss and travel the world for the rest of your life. So are you ready to create *F$CK YOU MONEY*? Before you answer "no" because you haven't quite hit your savings goal, here's the thing you need to know about the right time. It doesn't exist! Financial independence has always been about time, not money. If you view money as the goal, then you miss the point. To me, *F$CK YOU MONEY* simply meant having enough money so that I didn't have to worry about money and could finally follow my passions and find new passions. The most important thing to remember is there are many things money can buy, but the most valuable of all is freedom. And this is coming from the guy who retired before he hit his original financial target. Not enough to be considered a multi-millionaire according to traditional standards, but enough to say fuck you if needed. I'd been working on it long before I heard the term.

For those of you who have read my books, you already know you don't have to be the smartest person to have *F$CK YOU MONEY*. That's what this book is about. It is written to assist you in building your own. Why? Because you spend years working for others. They own you during this period. You get caught up in other people's games and waste time and energy that you will never get back. You start to respect your own ideas less and less by listening to so-called experts and conforming to conventional opinions. Without realizing it you've given up your independence...everything that makes you self reliant and entrepreneurial. Before it's too late, you must reassess your entire concept of *F$CK YOU MONEY*. It's not about possessing things, money or titles. You can have all of that in abundance, but if you are someone who looks to others for help, guidance or resources, then you will lose. *F$CK YOU MONEY* can only come from within. It comes from a disdain for anything or anybody that impinges upon your mobility. It comes from confidence in your decisions and from the best use of your time. Because if you don't own yourself first, you will continually be at the mercy of other people and circumstance, always looking outward instead of relying on yourself. Why? Because society offers you all kinds of crutches, experts to turn to, drugs to cure any psychological unease, mild pleasures to help pass or kill time and jobs to keep you just above water. For many it's hard to resist, and once you give in, it's like a prison that you can't leave. You continually look outward for help and this severely limits your options and maneuverability.

Well, I'm here to tell you that you can beat the game. This is your opportunity and it's hidden right out in the open. That is, if you only realize it. But, let me be clear. It's not easy, it's not quick and it takes time. Just like most goals worth striving for. So, I'm not here to make a show of false humility and modesty as if I got as far as I did by accident and not by ego and ambition. People create freedom in a variety of different ways. So unless you won the lottery or inherited a lot of money, you're probably in the same boat as everybody else. You're fighting for your life every day. You go to work and earn a living, you provide for your family and you try to have as much fun as you can along the way. But when your ambition and limitations come to a head, you have to make a decision. In today's world, this means developing a deliberate *F$CK YOU MONEY* mindset and attitude, and accruing the intangible benefits from doing so.

Everybody fantasizes about telling their boss to go fuck themselves, but Society has an incredible way of keeping you in check. This book is about the freedom that everybody longs for. Rising above the daily necessity to trade your time for money and living each day with a new sense of freedom, pride and self-determination. All of which helps you to build a mental equivalent of money, affluence, opulence and luxury. You will get a certain feeling, a certain mentality from it, because it breaks societal rules. It might not be what you're used to, but it has all of the elements to transform your relationship with money, in your ongoing quest to live your life exactly how you want. I'm just not giving it to you in the traditional packaging. Once you take the leap, you'll realize that it's not as difficult as you previously thought. And once you internalize the idea, it will put you in a position of power.

F$CK YOU MONEY

Function:

Noun

1. An infinite perpetuation of self-reliance.

2. The mental equivalent of money, affluence, opulence and luxury.

3. The courage to live a life true to yourself, not the life others expect of you.

4. Maintaining a desired lifestyle without needing employment or assistance from anyone.

5. Rejecting traditional social behavior and niceties of conduct without fear of consequences.

6. A strong measure of financial security that gives you options and makes you feel like you don't have to take shit from anyone.

F$CK YOU MONEY!

"You don't like how I'm living? Well, fuck you!"

~ Ice Cube

Introduction

IT'S CALLED F$CK YOU MONEY FOR A REASON

We all want to be "free," but what does that mean? Do you actively want to retire early, or are you content with working the traditional lifespan of a typical worker in our society? In 20 years, do you see yourself living in the same house? Working the same job? Driving the same car? What will change? Most people are trapped in a hierarchy where they have to ask permission to get what they want. A life that is defined by what people with power over us think is frustrating and can create pent up resentment, anger, and disappointment. But don't be swayed by social noise or by the financial success of others. If you want to live a unique and exceptional life, choose unique and exceptional things. I know it's easier said than done, but we live in a world of abundance. If you start giving yourself permission, you're not only helping yourself, you're helping your creativity, your productivity, your sanity, self-reliance, entrepreneurial mindset and sense of ownership.

I was living for the notion of assimilation of the American Dream that was being presented to me... the money, power, wealth and status, but that belief left me constantly broke and struggling to make ends meet. The most common mistake we make is looking outside of ourselves for what we can only find within. In reality, the problem was me. The problem was my mindset. I had to figure out a way to escape, look past the traditional, step over outdated methods and ignore the words "That's the way it has always been done." I believe that we should use our money to live our best lives according to our specific values and beliefs. It's never made sense to me to work your whole life and save all of the fun and enjoyment for the end when, you might not have the health or energy to do the things you want to do. So, the only solution I could come up with was to fuck up the program by living as a free man and designing a lifestyle that I would never want to retire from. The problem had always been that I thought I didn't have enough. But in reality, I had more than enough. I realized that I could leverage the money I already had. I didn't know it at the time, but I already had *F$CK YOU MONEY.*

F$CK YOU MONEY isn't about how wealthy you are it's simply a mindset and attitude choice. A mindset tool that allows you to leverage money that you control into highly valued experiences based on how you think. So when I talk about *F$CK YOU MONEY,* I'm really just asking you to listen to that voice inside of you. The true power of *F$CK YOU MONEY* lets us be our authentic selves without having to compromise our beliefs for money. This is standing tall and this is living as you should. For you are no longer a slave to your employer or business, but free and fully in charge of your life. You are now a person with options and a person with options lives on a higher plane. Practice acknowledging this attitude and mindset and choosing to act on thoughts centered around it. The more you do, the more you'll step into your truth and full potential. With that said, here is the reality: You can create *F$CK YOU MONEY* if you change your attitude and mindset and put an array of financial forces...all of which are within your control, into motion on your behalf. But, this book really isn't about *F$CK YOU MONEY.* It's about believing in yourself and taking the simple steps to transform your relationship with money in your ongoing quest to live your life exactly how you want. Your *F$CK YOU MONEY* mindset acts as kind of a mental safety net. When you are moving toward it, your mind snaps to attention, your energy is focused and intense and by by making yourself feel the necessity to create it, your mind will rise to the occasion. With your *F$CK YOU MONEY* attitude and mindset in hand and a path to financial independence set in stone, there will never be any regret. So pull the trigger and get started. When you come out on the other side it will all be worth it.

PART ONE

We can choose to use our attitude to change the world

RICH MOTHERF$CKER!

"Here's the dirty little secret about being rich. It's not about the money. It's about the way people see you, the way you see yourself. Fuck You Money!"

~ The Billionaire Boys Club

Chapter One

AUTHORITY NOT BASED ON MERIT, BUT ON SHEER POWER

(Act as a free man while surrounded by walls)

The person making $10 million per year believes they are going to do that. Because of their attitude, it's all they can see. The person making $50k per year believes that maybe $100k per year is the goal, but is really just limited by their own attitude and beliefs. Why not make 10 times what you're currently making? Why not have that be your belief? You can believe anything you want about money. Sit on that sentence for a minute and it might just change your life. It did for me when I first heard it. When I learned this I felt total freedom. The opinion you have of yourself is one of the most important keys to success. Confidence and self-esteem go a long way toward creating the mindset you need to create change and achieve your goals. Those who succeed in life do so because they view this attitude and all its resultant successes, achievements, influence and power as a positive and necessary thing. This cannot be overly stated. Ultimately, this book is about the mindset and attitude (not the money) that's required for the extraordinary to happen, so let's give it close attention. Why? Because you are simply hired help...a pawn in someone else's game. You show up at a certain time and bow down to authority. In essence you are exchanging money for freedom and this becomes the pattern for the rest of you life. Sooner or later, most people become miserable doing whatever it is they do for a living. The key is to foresee your misery so that by the time you are sick and tired of your current situation, you'll already have the financial literacy to make a change. This concept comes from looking at the world through the lens of *F$CK YOU MONEY*. From this simple metaphor we can draw much wisdom for improving our lives. You have to turn the dependence dynamic around, reverse this perspective and make everything work towards your own freedom and self-reliance. Again, it's not about possessing things, money or titles. It's about developing the mindset and attitude to give yourself the ultimate power.

Your goal in every maneuver in life must be ownership...no bosses above you. So many of us choose our path out of fear disguised as practicality. What we really want seems impossibly out of reach and ridiculous to expect, so we never even try. But, sometimes everything is suddenly really simple. Its like everything shifts in a moment and you step out of your body...out of your life. You step out and you clearly see where you really are. You see yourself and you think... fuck this shit!

HIERARCHY & YOUR PLACE WITHIN IT

The majority of people aren't advancing at the speed of which they are capable. Because they haven't discovered the self mastery of the *F$CK YOU MONEY* attitude, they lack personal power. This wrong thinking and weak will is preventing them from fully extending themselves toward their dreams. Money only matters if it helps you live a life you love. To reclaim our power, we must seek an immediate shift in attitude. This power begins with developing the mindset and attitude for real momentum. We can learn to master this role by practicing self examination. To some of you, this sounds like mere positive thinking, but who gives a damn? Should we continue to think negatively? Why think small when the impossible is capable.? This is a reachable possibility because the *F$CK YOU MONEY* mindset and attitude is simple to figure out and act upon. So let's begin the path by demystifying why we can do whatever we want to do.

I am a Black man born and raised in the United States. I have a *F$CK YOU MONEY* frame of reference and a *F$CK YOU MONEY* world view. I move through the world with a *F$CK YOU MONEY* experience. My experience is not a universal human experience. It is a particular experience in a society in which money and attitude about money matters profoundly. A society that is deeply separate and unequal by money. I was not taught to see myself in terms of money, but of course made aware that others' money mattered. Theirs, not mine. We make sense of our perceptions and experiences through our particular cultural lens. This lens is neither universal or objective. *F$CK YOU MONEY* holds that we are unique and stand apart from others and tells us that it is possible to be free of all bias. This ideology makes it possible to explore the collective aspects of the *F$CK YOU MONEY* experience. This mindset ensures that there are no intrinsic barriers to success and that failure is not a consequence, but a learning experience. When we grasp this idea of ourselves, we become more connected to the mindset and attitude of *F$CK YOU MONEY* in our lives. This must be our goal.

We know that to be defined as having *F$CK YOU MONEY* by the dominant culture is a different experience. Much of it is nonverbal and is achieved through watching and comparing ourselves to others. We gain our understanding and meaning collectively through aspects of the society around us, that are shared and unavoidable from television, movies, news, song lyrics, magazines, religion, traditions and so on. Our understanding of ourselves is based on our comparison to others and we come to understand who we are by understanding who we are not. To understand *F$CK YOU MONEY* we must push against our conditioning, in addition to challenging our sense of ourselves. So, right now you may be thinking of all the ways you are different from other people. I can predict that many readers will make precise claims of exception because we are products of our culture. So, I ask that you make specific adjustments you think are necessary to your situation rather than reject the evidence entirely. Your situation does not exempt you from the forces of *F$CK YOU MONEY* because no aspect of society is outside of these forces. Rather than use what you see about yourself as an exemption from further examination, a more fruitful approach would be to use your sense of uniqueness as a critical skill that will allow you to see the big picture of the society in which we live. Because we aren't raised to see ourselves in *F$CK YOU MONEY* terms, we position ourselves as unworthy of it. The defensiveness, denial and resistance runs deep. Acknowledging is only the first step, and this acknowledgment can be used in a way that allows us to figure out how *F$CK YOU MONEY* manifests itself in our daily lives and how it shapes our responses when challenged.

YOU HAVE BEEN FREED!
DON'T YOU UNDERSTAND?

In my own life, mediocrity and the status quo worked as a form of social coercion. I chose to avoid risk and conflict. Conversely when I accepted mediocrity, I was rewarded with social capital and viewed as the ultimate team player, but I didn't have freedom. I was raised in a society that taught me that there was no loss in my absence and that my absence was a good and desirable thing to be sought and maintained while simultaneously denying that fact. While there is a variation in how these messages are conveyed and how much we internalize them, nothing could have exempted me from the messages completely.

The practice of my life has been to align my life with the values I profess. Because I hadn't been socialized to see myself or to be seen by others as having *F$CK YOU MONEY,* today, because of my attitude and acquired mindset, I am free to move in virtually any space seen as valuable without worrying about class or status. In virtually every situation or context deemed prestigious in society, I belong. This belonging is a deep and ever-present mindset that has always been with me. *F$CK YOU MONEY* has settled deep into my consciousness. It shapes my daily thoughts and concerns...what I reach for in life and what I expect to find. *F$CK YOU MONEY* is so natural to me now that I don't even have to think about it. This attitude has shaped every aspect of my self-identity...my interests and investments...what I care about or don't care about...what I see or don't see...what I am drawn to and what I am repelled by... what I can take for granted...where I can go...how others respond to me and what I can ignore. It is this downright refusal to accept authority and a stubborn belief in myself that has gotten me this far in life.

The idea that *F$CK YOU MONEY* is limited only to certain people is the root of virtually all mediocrity and status-quo. To move beyond this mindset, we have to let go of this common belief. In a society in which *F$CK YOU MONEY* clearly matters, our attitude about it profoundly shapes us. If we want to challenge the status quo, we must make an honest accounting of how it manifests in our lives and in the society around us. Your *F$CK YOU MONEY* attitude deals with the impossibility and the possibility. Getting what you want out of life comes from an outrageously stubborn insistence that there is no other option. No matter how many times life says no, keep demanding what you want. In order to get to the money, you have to have the attitude.

"F$CK YOU MONEY" – EXERCISE APPENDIX - A

The standard of living you have is all because of the attitude and beliefs you have about yourself. What you believe about yourself determines all the results you have in your life regarding money. Most people have such a deep rooted, small view of themselves that they think money and wealth are out of reach for them. The truth is you can create any amount of wealth you want for yourself, you just have to have the right mindset and attitude for it. By answering the following questions and evaluating your current life experience, it will become clear as to whether or not your efforts are meaningful or whether you must set a new and more proactive course for your life.

- What am I really after in life? (money, freedom, love etc.)

- I believe I can make more money than I do now because?

- What steps can I take today, this week, this month, this year to make this happen?

- When I feel weak and distracted, the reason I will keep going is?

PART TWO

Accept nothing less than the absolute best out of life

F$CK YOU MONEY!

"Do ya'll ever get sick of being told exactly what to do? We some superstars. At least I am, and we should be able to do whatever we want to do."

~ Bobby Brown

Chapter Two

THE LUXURY, THE BIG TOYS & THE FANCY VACATIONS

(Elevate your lifestyle)

We all dream of living a luxurious life...michelin star restaurants, five-star hotels, exotic cars, yachts and luxury clothes. Doing what you want as opposed to doing what you feel obligated to do. Unfortunately, 99% of people are convinced that they are incapable of achieving great things, so they aim for the mediocre. Many think the dream is unattainable so they settle for less. We tend to think that everyone outside of our own socioeconomic status is some how smarter...better. Like the guy you see driving the Ferrari. He's only smarter because you think he is. He's not! But he does have something that you don't. That's why you picked up this book. This leads us to another equally important idea. One that most people implicitly refuse to accept...you have to give yourself permission to be free. I hear it all the time..."God I wish I could do what you do." My reply is always the same: "You can!" It's this process of gaining power over yourself that is the most satisfying of all, knowing that step-by-step you are elevating yourself above the dependent masses. So the question is, "How can you achieve the millionaire lifestyle of complete freedom without first having a million dollars?" Well, there is nothing wrong with desiring the finer things in life. In fact, I'm cheering for you. But, serious self-examination and decision-making are necessary to create the lifestyle that you want now, not later.

PERSONAL EXONERATION

I'm not a money coach...meaning I don't teach you how to budget, save or invest money. Instead, I teach you how to think like an entrepreneur and a business owner and tap into your attitude and mindset, to learn how to own and control your own life. Money just seems to follow. You must first learn how to think to attract a luxurious life, all of which can be achieved with little money in the bank. In fact, this attitude, not some money management system, is exactly how I got to *"THE LUXURY, THE BIG TOYS & THE FANCY VACATIONS."* A million dollars ($1,000,000) in the bank isn't the fantasy. The fantasy is the lifestyle of complete freedom it supposedly allows. It's a reversal of perspective because the term fuck you is generally a derogatory term that refers to people willing to do anything for themselves with no core values beyond promoting their own needs. For the purposes of this book however this is a misreading of the *F$CK YOU MONEY* phenomenon.

F$CK YOU MONEY is in fact a great art that comes with a belief system that is eminently positive and powerful. What it represents in today's society is a person who believes in their purpose and who doesn't need permission from any person or institution to live their lives on their own terms. If you look beyond a specific dollar amount, its simply a state of mind. One that you can acquire well in advance of your corresponding bank account and one that's founded so purely on your confidence in your self-reliance, that even if you lost all of your material possessions you'd still be happy because of your attitude. The first step is believing that *F$CK YOU MONEY* is bendable to our will. Those who lack this belief will never advance with great power because it's the perfect example of having your cake and eating it too and in my view, that is what *F$CK YOU MONEY* is all about.

THE MASTER OF THE
UNIVERSE WORKING HIS MAGIC

I get to choose how I exist in this world. I am a professor of entrepreneurship, self-reliance and the *F$CK YOU MONEY* attitude and it's the most confident I have ever felt in my entire motherfucking life. My attitude allows me to march to a distinctively different drummer. Instead of chasing millions I wanted to live a life that most millionaires would love to be living. But, as we grow up, we are always thinking about what's next and we end up rushing through life without stopping to really enjoy it. The more I thought about it, the stranger the notion of working my whole life to retire became. The whole premise of traditional retirement was faulty to me. Waiting until I was 65 when I would be less likely able or healthy enough to do the things I always wanted to do didn't make a lot of sense. I knew that if I didn't make moves I would regret it for the rest of my life. I had to step away from the typical routine and create a blank slate. How would I do that? By creating my own corner of the world. My *F$CK YOU MONEY* attitude would allow me to play the game of money by my own rules, travel the world in style and live a life of freedom, prosperity and financial control. My plan was to form a system of distributors to sell my concept nationally and to travel internationally... the goal was fun and profit.

Let me pause here for a moment because I want to make a major disclaimer. In my previous books *BAD A$$ CEO* and *RICH MOTHERF$CKER*, I taught you how to free yourself from financial slavery, taught you that if you eliminate debt, you'll have the cash flow to rapidly build wealth and most importantly, I told you that there is a concerted effort being waged against you to take the wealth that you will produce over a lifetime away from you by using credit. So, what I'm about to share with you breaks traditional barriers and goes against what you've previously been taught. I'm not telling you to do exactly what I do, but sharing my methods. If you choose to use any of these methods, please proceed with extreme caution and only do what's best for your situation. As I have done in all of my books, this is where I pull the curtain back on my lifestyle and show you how you can join me.

Because I taught you how to free yourself from financial slavery and eliminate debt, I want to let you know that capitalizing on great credit doesn't have to mean incurring new debt. I use credit cards to pay for almost everything I buy, but I haven't paid a lick of interest on a credit card in years, while earning hundreds of thousands of reward points that I transfer into airline miles or hotel rooms, that I book for pennies on the dollar. Using points and miles to book these flights has allowed me to travel the world in style being treated like royalty, fly in total comfort in first or business class in a lie flat bed in the sky, eating lobster and sipping on champagne. Not the cheap stuff either, but Krug and Dom Perignon. I have saved thousands on flights to Thailand (twice)...damn I love Bangkok; South Africa, Brazil, France, China, Singapore (twice), Austalia and Japan to name a few. Traveling to these places is great, but for me the flights there and back are even more important than the destination. Knowing that you will be flying in the best seat, eating the best food on the plane, and being treated like a king, gives you the feeling of importance and status, fundamentally recognizing that no matter how much a trip did or didn't cost, money is no object when it comes to purchasing power when strategically using points. But it doesn't stop there. As a businessman, I tend to be obsessed with numbers and ROI. I have innate instincts for getting the best possible deal out of everything in life. So I stay at five star hotels exclusively and take the luxury hotel and resort experience thing to the extreme. Once I arrive I can check in early if I need to, I am automatically upgraded, my wi-fi is complimentary, my wife and I receive breakfast daily during our stay, I don't have to rush when it's time for me to leave because I don't have to check out until 4pm and I relish in my VIP status because the hotel gives me a complimentary spa or food and beverage credit.

And all of this is guaranteed. First and business class flights and 5-star hotels are the only ones that are worthy of me and I use them as an ROI-based decision. For me, they serve as a kind of reverse investment. Like I said earlier, I am able to do this by converting my credit card points into airline miles and pay for hotel rooms. Without logging millions of miles a year in the air, I earn points through credit card sign up bonuses and my everyday spending. By effectively monetizing the inner calculus of rewards travel, the airlines and hotels essentially work for me. Empowered by a new-found sense of consumer leverage and your *F$CK YOU MONEY* mindset and attitude they can work for you too. So, let's think outside the box a little bit so you can learn how to leverage the system, upgrade your travel experience and travel the world like a millionaire using points and miles.

STEP ONE: USE MY BOOKS BAD A$$ CEO & RICH MOTHERF$CKER TO BECOME DEBT FREE

This chapter is about traveling with points, but this book is about *F$CK YOU MONEY* so if you are fiscally responsible you have a real opportunity to win at the expense of credit card companies. In my previous books, I taught you that if you eliminate debt, you'll have the cash flow to rapidly build wealth and in the right hands, a good credit rating can be a real asset. If you're in debt, don't start trying to rack up points. Get out of debt first. Leveraging credit and traveling the world like a millionaire works best for people who don't need to borrow a dime and pay their credit card balances in full every month. Hundreds of thousands or even millions of points and miles are available to those who are fiscally responsible with credit. If you're going to play this game, only do so without the risk of falling into financial ruin.

STEP TWO: DECIDE HOW YOU WANT TO TRAVEL

Like I shared with you earlier, I like to travel the world in style in first or business class, be treated like royalty, eat lobster and sip champagne while flying in total comfort in a lie flat bed in the sky. The thought of flying 12 hours in coach doesn't in any way align with my *F$CK YOU MONEY* mindset and attitude. For me the goal isn't always the lowest cost. I redeem points and miles for high-value experiences and focus on aspirational travel to gain access to $20,000 first class airfare and stay in $1,100 per night hotel rooms that I would never otherwise pay for. Take a step back and think about what kind of traveler you are. Not in terms of how you've been traveling, but in the context of how you want to travel and figure out what works for you.

STEP THREE: SIGN UP FOR AIRLINE & HOTEL LOYALTY PROGRAMS

The cornerstone of traveling like a millionaire and using points and miles, is to maintain multiple loyalty program accounts. As your balances build up over time, you'll be able to redeem the miles and points for valuable rewards all over the world. With some hotel chains you can apply both your hotel rewards number and an airline program to your stay, earning both points and miles. Do some research and figure out which programs are best for your specific travel goals and destinations based on how you decide to travel and sign up for accounts with all the loyalty programs that are relevant to you. Virtually all of these programs are free to join and every time you fly or stay at a hotel, make sure you use your number. Never board an airplane or stay at a hotel without providing a frequent flyer or hotel loyalty program number.

STEP FOUR: CHOOSE YOUR TRAVEL REWARD CREDIT CARDS

The fastest way to obtain hundreds of thousands of points quickly is through credit card sign-up bonuses and in my opinion, transferring points for international, first and business class cabin redemptions are the best use of miles. Depending on the card, you can earn 50,000, 60,000 or even 100,000 points after spending between $3000 and $5000 within the first three months after activating the card. Before applying for a card or even the thought of a trip, I am strategically planning how I can get the best value and return on my investment. The idea is to hack the system and use credit cards and rewards programs against themselves, to get a lot of points and miles without spending a lot of money. Most points/miles are earned on the ground. You don't have to fly a lot or stay in hotels to earn points and miles. The majority of my points are earned before I ever get on a plane or check into a hotel, by paying my monthly bills. I earn 6 points for every dollar spent at hotels, 5 points for every dollar spent at restaurants and on airfare, 4 points for every dollar spent on gas and 2 points for every dollar spent for everything else. I don't make even a single purchase without considering the points/miles earning implications. You don't need to spend any money outside of your everyday spending to earn these points and miles, so don't spend outside of your means. It's not about spending a lot of money, but once you have the right cards, you want to do everything you can to put all your spending on them to reach the minimum spend required for the sign up bonus, or if you just want to earn more miles and points for an award.

The real art of traveling like a millionaire by using points/miles is not just in collecting points, but in redeeming them. I learned that points can be worth more when used to book international first and business class airline tickets, so as an entrepreneur and an author, my travel strategy is to research Skytrax world airline awards to determine which airlines have the top five first or business class seats, so I can ascertain which seat I will book with points/miles to enhance the luxury and comfort of my trip. More than anything, I do this so I can get the best of the best, but not have to pay for expensive hotel suites or $20,000 for a first class seat, but still enjoy the experience. There is no right or wrong way to do this. Just figure out what works for you. Decide what you want to use the points for, get the best credit card(s) you can, then, charge everything and anything to that card and pay it off every month. Be careful not to over spend just to hit the minimum purchase requirement to get the reward. Think of your points and your miles like your stock or retirement accounts and treat your credit like an asset. It's about using the money you are already spending and a credit card or cards for a *F$CK YOU MONEY* advantage.

BOLD & UNAPOLOGETIC

This is what I love doing...traveling, informing and empowering. Your *F$CK YOU MONEY* mindset and attitude represent possibility... that there is an another way for you to be in the world, other than the way the world has dictated you have to be. I have traveled to over 19 countries by using the methods I share in this book. My goal is to maximize every trip and make the most of my adventures. Traveling like this can be a particularly rewarding way to live a life of luxury without a big budget, since you get unique once-in-a-lifetime experiences. The way I see it, this was all made possible by my inclination to say fuck you and do what is right for me. Now I will admit that this disposition has sometimes lead me in a direction that is not genuinely best for me, but the radical change it brought into my life has been incredibly beneficial. If you don't have the proper *F$CK YOU MONEY* mindset and attitude in your given circumstance, go find it. It's all about using your perspective to gain an outcome in your favor, so live as a free man/woman and make *F$CK YOU MONEY* an absolute in your life. Those of us with a *F$CK YOU MONEY* mindset and attitude don't give a damn if anybody approves. We don't seek permission from the world because we know the world is bound by mediocrity and will never approve anything that breaks convention. We don't need a certificate or a letter of recommendation...we simply take action. All that means is that I don't have to do what I don't want to do. Having *F$CK YOU MONEY* is the logical extreme of a certain conception of American freedom... complete ownership over yourself and your time. People who have a solid sense of their own value and who feel secure about themselves have a capacity to look at the world with greater objectivity. *F$CK YOU MONEY* answers with strength and readiness to defend and fight for your dreams. I don't want to be told how to live my life. I want to chart my own course, one that means something to me in my way... I want to pursue and experience the best in the world. The irony is that, in many situations, having a *F$CK YOU MONEY* mindset and attitude is exactly the path that leads you there.

"F$CK YOU MONEY" – EXERCISE APPENDIX - B

You can significantly upgrade your travel experiences through strategic use of airline miles, hotel points and credit card rewards. I've been able to travel to amazing places in a style I would never have thought possible by maximizing the value of my mindset. The difference is in the possibilities that are created by leveraging your *F$CK YOU MONEY* attitude and with the right points/miles, mindset and attitude, anything is possible. Based on the places you're hoping to visit and how you'd like to get there, here are the tips I recommend.

- Figure out what kind of traveler you are (Economy, Business or First class).

- Decide where you want to go.

- Sign up for loyalty programs

- Make sure you're ready to handle the financial responsibility of paying your balances off every month.

- Apply for credit cards.

- Leverage every opportunity to build points/miles.

- Rather than using cash, put even small charges on your credit card.

- Track your spending carefully so you know exactly how much you need to spend to get the points you need.

- Read the Travel hacking blogs (Points Guy, One Mile at a Time, God Save the Points etc.).

- Convert your points/miles into flights and hotel stays.

- Make sure that you earn points on all travel (flights, hotels, rental cars, etc.) by entering your loyalty program membership number.

There are a lot of variables here, but none of this is set in stone. Think about the trip you want to take, where you want to stay and how you want to get there. Points and miles can help you see the world in style.

PART THREE

The privilege of membership

F$CK YOU MONEY!

"You are never going to rise above where you are until you rise above who you are."

~ Iyanla Vanzant

Chapter Three

LONG LIVE THE KING

(Open the door to a world of privilege)

I know what it's like to be free. If my life ended today, I would tell you it was an incredible life and that I drew great joy from the study and the struggle toward freedom which I urge you. You have seen that the struggle has ruptured and remade me several times over. The changes have awarded me the ecstasy of freedom that comes only when you can no longer be lied to because you reject other peoples vision of the American Dream and only accept your own. Why? Because I had repeatedly been told that what I wanted to achieve was unrealistic, unreasonable and often just downright silly. The American Dream was a rock floating in another galaxy, around another sun, in another sky that I would never get to. I always thought that I had to mirror the outside world, create a carbon copy, but, it became clear that the dream concocted by society was to justify itself, so I had to conjure up my own dreams, to replace what was constantly being presented to me. It occurred to me that in order to be free, I had to question the logic of the dream itself. The affluence that surrounds us has been called the American dream and with good reason, because we've been asleep. We wake up by questioning the dream. This theory relieved me of certain troubling questions and this was the starting point of my *F$CK YOU MONEY* mindset...the hardest, sharpest sword you could imagine. I wasn't just motivated, I was driven. I had to save myself from what seemed to be the unbridgeable distance between me and my freedom. The story of my own royalty became a weapon for me. That was the kind of power I sought. It became an obsession I couldn't shake.

Today I am the King...I don't care how much it appears otherwise. *F$CK YOU MONEY* doesn't have to show off. It is confident, self-assuring, self-starting, self-stopping and self-justifying. When you have it, you know it. Those are the facts. I have proven to myself that there was another way and I'm in control. I have seen other worlds and expanded my notion of the *F$CK YOU MONEY* spectrum and I had to be strong and purposeful to get where I am. I had to wait, plan and look around. Now I am here and I am going to stay because after you win the game, you take the prize, keep it, and protect it. I know of no other way of living...no other forms of success available to me. This is not boasting...it is a declaration of freedom.

Do you know who you really are and what you're capable of? Are you taking enough bold and significant action in order to advance your life and reach your full potential? We all make habitual, self-limiting choices. No matter who you are, where you live, what you do for a living or how much money you make, you're probably living at about 40 percent of your true capability. That's a damn shame because we all have the potential to be so much more. The only way we can change is to be real with ourselves, because the person you see in the mirror everyday is going to reveal the truth. This is about taking the first step to becoming the real you. If you were unafraid and acting from your highest self, what would you be doing to move forward in life? What do you need to do today...this week, to start dramatically living the life you desire? There's something to be said about living it instead of just reading about it. Anybody can become a totally different person and achieve what so-called experts like to claim as impossible, because your idea of F$CK YOU MONEY can only come from you. It is a requisite inner strength and an exercise that you must practice on a daily basis, but people won't like your boldness. They will call your struggles crazy. There will be resistance from some who see you moving forward without their permission, or without them. This is a reality that must be faced by all those who strive to obtain a *F$CK YOU MONEY* mindset and attitude and who seek to realize their dreams.

When I was searching for F$CK YOU MONEY, I would write about it. In my writings, I had to answer a series of questions. Throughout my books, I have given you these same assignments. These were the earliest acts of personal interrogation that drew me into consciousness and the revelation of the following principles:

THE POWER OF
NOT GIVING A FUCK

✓ F$CK YOU MONEY cannot be taken for granted!

✓ F$CK YOU MONEY is clear about what it wants and why!

✓ F$CK YOU MONEY loudly proclaims its love of freedom!

✓ F$CK YOU MONEY is a natural resource of incomparable value!

✓ F$CK YOU MONEY means living freely by crafting a life on our own terms!

✓ F$CK YOU MONEY comes with a belief system that is eminently positive and powerful!

✓ F$CK YOU MONEY is not an indefinable mass of flesh. It is a particular, specific mindset and attitude!

- ✓ F$CK YOU MONEY turns its favor toward those who take action, awarding them with success and recognition in life!

- ✓ F$CK YOU MONEY tells you that against all evidence and odds, you are the master of your own life!

- ✓ F$CK YOU MONEY thrives on generalization not on limiting possibilities and immediate privileged answers!

F$CK YOU MONEY is an experience of freedom at a psychological level. You are free from the slavery of unconsciously held assumptions about money and free from the guilt, resentment, envy, frustration and despair you may have felt about money issues. When you have a *F$CK YOU MONEY* mindset and attitude, the way money functions in your life is determined by you, not your circumstances. In this way, money isn't something that happens to you, it's something that you include in your life in a purposeful way. *F$CK YOU MONEY* is complex and nuanced and its manifestations are not the same for everyone. It's another way of declaring yourself. To challenge this ideology, we must suspend our perception of ourselves and develop the ability to see yourself with *F$CK YOU MONEY*. Why? Because everyone wants to walk through a door marked private...to gain the privilege of membership and therefore have a reason to feel affluent. To live without a *F$CK YOU MONEY* mindset and attitude is to be naked before the elements of the world. The truth is, I owe my *F$CK YOU MONEY* mindset everything I have. Before it, I had nothing. I recall learning these principles clearer than learning my shapes and colors because these principles were essential to my economic empowerment. What I want for you is to grow into this consciousness because the truth is, we can will ourselves to an escape of our own.

That is the hope of this movement. To awaken your *F$CK YOU MONEY* mindset, so that you can live free because there is so much out there to live for. Not just playing someone else's game, but by playing your own game within the game.

THE EXTRAVAGANT
THEATER OF FUCK YOU

From the time you take your first breath, you become eligible to die. You also become eligible to find your greatness. In a society where mediocrity is too often the standard and too often rewarded, there is intense fascination with people who detest mediocrity, who refuse to define themselves in conventional terms and who seek to transcend traditionally recognized capabilities. This is exactly the type of person you are meant to be. An old adage says we should live every day as if it were our last. It's the small things in life that add up to create the big picture. Each of us has the opportunity, when it comes to contributing to the space we are a part of and we should see this as a gift and a blessing. *F$CK YOU MONEY* translates to seize the day. It tells us to put aside our differences, fears and worries, prioritize what really matters and just go for it. We all have amazing stories to tell and we should love to share them. It's these little bits of what I like to call rebelliousness that create these pages that I know will inspire you.

I proposed to take my claims of *F$CK YOU MONEY* exceptionalism seriously, which is to say I proposed to subject myself to an exceptional standard of living. Great leaders are excellent at creating a vision and a strategy, then motivating others toward turning that vision into tangible realities. If you are a fan of the *BAD BOYS FINI$H RICH* series of books, then you know that the words fuck you set me on a path to success. There is something spiritual about getting up every morning and knowing that whatever I do today is because I made the choice to do it...*F$CK YOU MONEY!* That's pretty cool huh? If that appeals to you, then this was definitely the book for you. My goal is to always provide you with an unforgettable experience, but never forget that I am a Capitalist...so at a nominal fee of course. My work is to give you what I know of my own particular path while allowing you to walk your own. But, this can be difficult for you because all around us there exists a powerful apparatus urging us to accept mediocrity at face value and not inquire about freedom. Choosing our own aims and seeking to bring them to fruition creates a sense of vitality and motivation in life. Only you can master your mindset and attitude, which is what it takes to live a bold life filled with accomplishments that most people consider beyond their capability. So, I tell you now that the question of how one should live within the context of *F$CK YOU MONEY* ultimately answers itself. I have told you what my mentor in the mirror told me: "Find out who you really are and learn to live at your fullest potential. This is your world, this is your dream and you must live intentionally and independently, manifesting a freer life. Everything else is wishing and hoping. "

HEIR TO EVERYTHING

In our rapidly changing economic environment, the spirit of *F$CK YOU MONEY* has come before you. The groundwork has been laid for your progress and future success. It provides an opportunity for each of you to compete at the highest level...to rewrite the rules of the game. If you grasp the mindset and attitude, you'll know how the new game can be played. So where do you go from here? Well, If there is one thing I can tell you that's true, it's that people don't attempt to control people who don't give a fuck, because that action takes their power away. It's simple psychology. We are taught to wait our turn, not rock the boat and stay the course. We were taught this storybook perfect behavior in school, on our jobs and at home. However, we don't learn *F$CK YOU MONEY* skills in any institutionalized setting. This type of self-imprisonment is the greatest misconception and weakness of many as they struggle through life and these rules of behavior govern the lives of many people today. It's a form of psychological slavery...controlled through intimidation and propaganda.

If you are trapped in this society of duplicity, do you try to opt out or do you assimilate? It's unfortunate that so many people see life as an occurrence guided by a mystical existence and not by the choices they make. You see, when you get to a point of not giving a fuck, you have a vision to pursue...a calling to accomplish and a destiny to encounter. Having a *F$CK YOU MONEY* mindset and attitude is essential to achieving success in any scenario because the perception of not being able to be bullshitted because you know who you are and where you stand is extremely powerful.

Now let me be clear with you. I'm not telling you to be an asshole. As I stated earlier, *F$CK YOU MONEY* simply makes the seemingly impossible become possible. Everyone is seeking a route to follow on this journey of life. Often, individuals spend hours and days, that turn into months and years, trying to figure out what to do with their life. They devise vague or fruitless goals. They express their desire to live in a larger house, drive an expensive car and travel like the rich and famous. They always fall short in gaining these things because they wrongly focus upon these ideals with the wrong attitude and mindset. It's not about the money, it's about the mentality that you will gain from the investment, so the following rules should govern your behavior:

- F$CK YOU MONEY is a sport, play it!

- F$CK YOU MONEY is education, learn it!

- F$CK YOU MONEY is a mystery, solve it!

- F$CK YOU MONEY is the goal, achieve it!

- F$CK YOU MONEY is a venture, invest in it!

- F$CK YOU MONEY is a mission, act upon it!

- F$CK YOU MONEY is an opportunity, seize it!

- F$CK YOU MONEY is an adventure, experience it!

F$CK YOU MONEY is freedom. It's not something you receive from someone, it is an internal empowerment, solely achieved by your choices in life. It's not granted to you, it is created by you. So, seize opportunities as they are presented or invented and face new, adventures with courage, a reasonable knowledge of the subject matter and a vision of the outcome. Your *F$CK YOU MONEY* mindset and attitude present unique opportunities that you must capture. This calling is your destiny. Don't wait for *F$CK YOU MONEY* to come to you...you must take action to create it. When you do, you will play the game of money by your own rules, travel the world in style and live a life of freedom, prosperity and financial control.

BE A PART OF THE THOUSANDS OF LIVES CHANGED WITH THE HELP OF THE BAD BOYS FINI$H RICH PRINCIPLES!

Here's How It Works:

1. Once you receive your book, create a video of you holding up the book and enthusiastically saying the following:

I'm (First & Last Name) from (City & State or City and Country)!
"Bad Boys or Bad Girls" Finish Rich! (Based on your gender)
I Got My Copy, Get Yours!

2. Post the video on Social media (youtube.com, instagram, facebook etc.)

3. Email the link of your video to admin@badboysfinishrich.com.

Once we receive your video link and verify it for clarity and authenticity, we will add it to our growing list of videos.

Please Note: Please follow the script provided above. We reserve the right to reject and refuse any videos deemed substandard or inappropriate.

Visit **BADBOYSFINISHRICH.COM**
for examples!

BAD BOYS FINI$H RICH

BOLD AMBITION
WORLDWIDE

www.ingramcontent.com/pod-product-compliance
Lightning Source LLC
Chambersburg PA
CBHW071121210326
41519CB00020B/6380